TORONTO PUBLIC LIBRARY

Countries of the World: A Primary Source Journey

A Primary Source Guide to
SPAIN

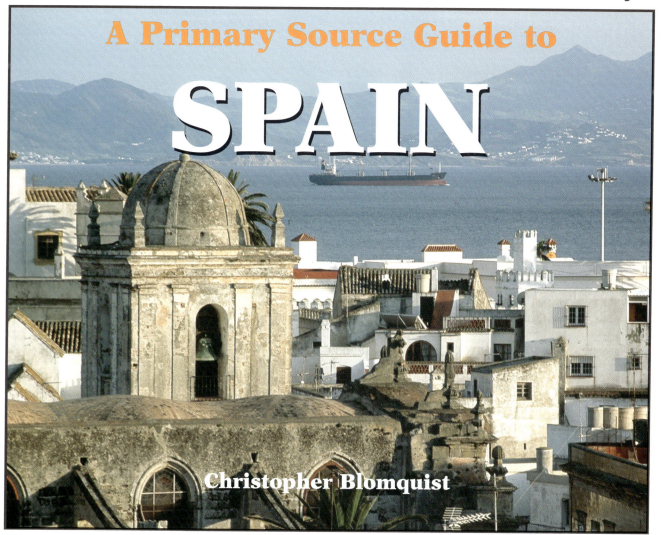

Christopher Blomquist

New York

For Andrea, John, John Felipe, and Anna Quatrale: una familia fabulosa

Published in 2005 by The Rosen Publishing Group, Inc.
29 East 21st Street, New York, NY 10010

Copyright © 2005 by The Rosen Publishing Group, Inc.

All rights reserved. No part of this book may be reproduced in any form without permission in writing from the publisher, except by a reviewer.

First Edition

Editor: Kathy Kuhtz Campbell
Book Design: Haley Wilson
Layout Design: Michael J. Caroleo

Photo Credits: Cover, p. 1 © Miguel Gonzalez/Laif/Aurora Photos; p. 4 © 2002 GeoAtlas; p. 6 © Eddie Soloway/Getty Images; p. 6 (inset) © Martin Child/SuperStock, Inc.; p. 8 © AKG; p. 8 (inset) © Peter Bowater/Photo Researchers; p. 10 © Erich Lessing/Art Resource, NY; p. 10 (inset) © Robert Capa/Magnum Photos; p. 11 © Scala/Art Resource, NY; p. 12 © Bettmann/Corbis; p. 13 © AFP/Corbis; p.14 © Jan-Peter Lanall/Peter Arnold, Inc.; p. 14 (inset) © Larry Mangino/The Image Works; p.16 © Patrick Ward/Corbis; p. 18 (top) © Archivo Iconografico, S.A./Corbis; p.18 (bottom) © 2003 Estate of Pablo Picasso/Artists Rights Society (ARS), New York/photo © Erich Lessing/Art Resource, NY; p. 19 © Victoria and Albert Museum, London/Art Resource, NY; p. 20 © Jose Fuste Raga/Corbis; p. 20 (inset) © Reuters NewMedia Inc./Corbis.

Library of Congress Cataloging-in-Publication Data

Blomquist, Christopher.
A primary source guide to Spain / Christopher Blomquist.
   p. cm. — (Countries of the world, a primary source journey)
Summary: Introduces the history, government, geography, and culture of Spain, along with other information about this European nation. Includes bibliographical references and index.
ISBN 1-4042-2757-1 (lib. bdg.)
1. Spain—Juvenile literature. [1. Spain.] I. Title. II. Series.
DP17 .B56 2005
946—dc22
                              2003015717

Manufactured in the United States of America

Contents

Looking at Spain 5
A Land of Mountains 7
España 9
A World Power, for a While 11
Spain's Government 13
The Spanish Economy 15
A Very Catholic Country 17
Gifted Artists and Writers 19
Spain Today 21
Spain at a Glance 22
Glossary 23
Index 24
Primary Source List 24
Web Sites 24

Looking at Spain

Spain is the second-largest country in western Europe after France. Spain's land, including its islands and territories, covers 195,364 square miles (505,990 sq km). Spain lies in southwestern Europe on the Iberian **Peninsula**. Mountains in the northeast called the Pyrenees separate Spain from the rest of Europe.

Spain makes up about four-fifths of the peninsula. The remaining one-fifth is Portugal, Spain's neighbor to the west. Spain's neighbors to the northeast are France and the tiny country of Andorra. Morocco, in northern Africa, is just 9 miles (14.5 km) south of Spain. The narrow waterway called the Strait of Gibraltar flows between the Iberian Peninsula and Morocco.

Among the areas under Spain's control are the Moroccan cities of Ceuta and Melilla. The Balearic Islands off Spain's eastern coast and the Canary Islands, which are southwest of Spain in the Atlantic Ocean, also belong to Spain.

A Land of Mountains

The broad, flat land in the center of Spain is called the Meseta. It is 77,000 square miles (199,429 sq km) in area. The Meseta is surrounded by two rings of mountains and two **basins**. The Ebro Basin is in the northeast and the Guadalquivir Basin is in the southeast.

The tallest peak on the Spanish mainland, or the part of Spain located on the peninsula, is Mulhacén in the Sierra Nevada range. It rises to 11,421 feet (3,481 m). Pico de Teide in the Canary Islands is Spain's highest point. This peak rises 12,198 feet (3,718 m) above the sea. In Europe, only Switzerland has more mountains than Spain has.

◀ The Spanish Pyrenees are a natural border between France and Spain. Spain is a land of many mountains but few rivers. *Inset*: Spain's capital, Madrid, is located on the Meseta. Madrid reaches more than 100°F (40°C) in the summer.

España

Humans lived in Spain about 700,000 years ago. About 15,000 years ago, they painted animals on the walls of the Altamira Cave in the north. From 1100 B.C. to A.D. 414, many peoples **invaded** Spain. These included Phoenicians, Greeks, Celts, Carthaginians, Romans, and Visigoths. Today Spaniards call Spain España. This name may have come from the Romans. They called the peninsula Hispania, which means "hidden," because the mountain and ocean borders separated settlements from other lands.

In A.D. 711, Moors from northern Africa invaded southern Spain. They brought their religion, called **Islam**, and **culture** with them.

Early humans created this painting of a bison, an animal similar to a buffalo, in the Altamira Cave. Inset: The Alhambra in Granada was the last Moorish stronghold in Spain. Catholic armies drove the Moors from Spain in 1492.

A World Power, for a While

Spain's **Age of Exploration** began when King Ferdinand V and Queen Isabella I paid for the ocean journeys of Italian explorer Christopher Columbus. Columbus landed in the Americas in 1492. Spain became a mighty world power in the 1500s, thanks to explorers such as Francisco Pizarro and Hernán Cortés, who set up Spanish colonies in the Americas. However, Spain began to lose wars and colonies. France invaded Spain from 1808 to 1814. In 1898, the United States won lands in the Spanish-American War. In 1939, General Francisco Franco took over Spain's government and turned it into a **dictatorship**.

Spain's navy, called the Armada, was the most powerful until England's navy destroyed it in 1588. *Inset*: Soldiers such as this one fought against General Franco's forces in the Spanish Civil War (1936–1939). *Above*: In 1493, King Ferdinand and Queen Isabella gave Columbus this family banner.

Spain's Government

Juan Carlos I became king of Spain after the dictator Francisco Franco died in 1975. King Juan Carlos quickly made the government more **democratic**. In 1978, Spaniards voted for a **constitution**, and it was adopted that year. Spaniards elect a **parliament** called the General Courts. This group has two parts, the Congress of Deputies and the Senate. Deputies choose the prime minister. Senators act for Spain's 17 regions. Today the king advises the government. Spain's prime minister runs the government and has more power than the king.

◄ In 1975, Juan Carlos I took an oath to become king. Under Franco's rule, Spaniards had lost many civil rights. Juan Carlos I has worked to return democracy to Spaniards. *Above*: José Maria Aznar Lopez became Spain's prime minister in 1996.

The Spanish Economy

Spain's economy has grown quickly since Spain joined the **European Union** in 1986. Spain continues to modernize its factories and businesses. In January 2002, Spain adopted the European Union's euro as its official currency. The euro replaced the peseta.

Spain's main crops include grains, olives, grapes, oranges, and other fruits. Spain manufactures automobiles, cloth, and shoes, among other products. Many of Spain's factories are located on the southern coasts or in big cities such as Madrid and Seville. **Tourism** is an important, and growing, source of money for Spain.

About 6 million tourists come every year to the beaches of Majorca, the largest island in the Balearic Islands. In 1999, Spain made $32.9 billion from tourism. *Inset:* A farmer harvests olives near Madrid. *Above:* In 2002, the euro replaced the peseta as Spain's money.

A Very Catholic Country

More than 90 percent of the Spanish population is Roman Catholic. Roman Catholicism used to be the official religion of Spain. Today, because of the 1978 constitution, Spain offers religious freedom to all. The other religions practiced in Spain include some Protestant faiths, Judaism, and Islam.

Most Spaniards believe religious holidays are very important. Semana Santa, or Holy Week, is honored across Spain. It is held each spring from Palm Sunday through Easter Sunday. Seville is known for its Semana Santa festival. Men march in Seville's streets wearing hoods and carrying candles and decorated *pasos*, which are floats with holy images on them.

◀ In Seville, people take part in Semana Santa. They wear black clothing and hoods and carry lighted candles as part of the holy procession. More than 50 churches in this southern Spanish city take part in the processions.

Top: This is the 1605 title page of Cervantes's *Don Quixote*. *Don Quixote* is considered the greatest work in Spanish writing.

Gifted Artists and Writers

Some important artists have lived and worked in Spain. Diego Velázquez lived from 1599 to 1660. Franciso José de Goya lived from 1746 to 1828. Pablo Picasso lived from 1881 to 1973. Madrid's Prado Museum shows hundreds of the world's major artworks.

Spain has many great writers. Miguel de Cervantes wrote Spain's most famous book, *Don Quixote*, which was first printed in the 1600s. It is about a man who thinks he is a knight and has adventures. Since 1904, five Spanish writers have won the **Nobel Prize**. They are José Echegaray, Jacinto Benavente, Juan Ramón Jiménez, Vincente Aleixandre, and Camilo José Cela.

◀ Picasso's *Guernica* of 1937 shows his anger over an attack on the town of Guernica during the Spanish Civil War. *Above:* Goya made the print *The Sleep of Reason Produces Monsters* in 1797–98.

Spain Today

Today's Spain is filled with adventure. After bearing the pain of the Spanish Civil War and Franco's hard rule, Spaniards are now showing the rest of the world that their country is in much better spirits. The Guggenheim Museum in Bilbao may be the best symbol of the country's changed attitude. The museum, which opened in 1997, is shiny, bright, and fun to visit, just as Spain is.

Although Spain is ready for the future, it is not letting go of its favorite **traditions**. Spanish soccer teams such as Real Madrid and FC Barcelona are among the world's best teams. Other Spanish traditions include watching bullfights and dancing the **flamenco**.

Bilbao's Guggenheim Museum houses modern art. Many people think the museum looks like a giant silver fish. *Inset:* The running of the bulls in Pamplona in July starts the bullfighting season. Bulls that are to fight that day are let out into the streets. People show bravery by running ahead of the bulls to the bullring.

Spain at a Glance

Population: 40,077,100
Capital City: Madrid, population 2,882,860
Largest City: Madrid
Official Name: Kingdom of Spain
National Anthem: "Marcha Real" ("Royal March")
Land Area: 195,364 square miles (505,990 sq km)
Government: Parliamentary monarchy
Unit of Money: Euro
Flag: Spain's flag has a red stripe on top, a yellow stripe that is twice as wide in the middle, and another red stripe on the bottom. Spain's **coat of arms** appears in the flag's yellow stripe. It shows the Spanish royal seal between two columns. The two columns stand for Gibraltar and Ceuta.

Glossary

Age of Exploration (AYJ UV ek-spluh-RAY-shun) A time in the 1500s and 1600s when Europeans searched and colonized the Americas.

basins (BAY-sinz) Areas of land on either side of a river.

coat of arms (KOHT UV ARMZ) The special seal of some person, family, or ruling body.

constitution (kon-stih-TOO-shun) The basic rules by which a country is governed.

culture (KUL-chur) The beliefs, practices, and arts of a group of people.

democratic (deh-muh-KRA-tik) Having to do with a government that is run by the people who live under it.

dictatorship (dik-TAY-ter-ship) A government run by one person.

European Union (yur-uh-PEE-in YOON-yun) A group of countries in Europe that work together to be friendly and to better their economies.

flamenco (flah-MEN-koh) A dance brought to the Spanish region of Andalusia by a group of people called Gypsies.

invaded (in-VAYD-ed) Entered a place in order to attack and take over.

Islam (IS-lom) A faith based on Mohammed's teachings and the Koran.

Nobel Prize (noh-BEL PRYZ) An award of money given each year to a person or a group for working in a subject, such as writing.

parliament (PAR-lih-mint) The lawmakers of a country.

peninsula (peh-NIN-suh-luh) Land surrounded by water on three sides.

tourism (TUR-ih-zem) A business serving those who travel for pleasure.

traditions (truh-DIH-shunz) Ways of doing things that have been passed down over time.

Index

A
Age of Exploration, 11
Altamira Cave, 9

C
Cervantes, Miguel de, 19
Cortés, Hernán, 11

F
Ferdinand V, king of Spain, 11
Franco, Francisco, 11, 13

G
Goya, Francisco José de, 19

I
Isabella I, queen of Spain, 11
Islam, 9

J
Juan Carlos I, king of Spain, 13

M
Meseta, the, 7

Moors, 9
Mulhacén, 7

P
parliament, 13
Picasso, Pablo, 19
Pico de Teide, 7
Pizarro, Francisco, 11

S
soccer teams, 21
Spanish-American War, 11

Primary Source List

Page 8. Painting of a wisent, also called a bison, from Altamira Cave, in Cantabria, northern Spain. Early humans created the paintings of bison, wild boar, horses, and other animals on the ceiling of the cave around 10,000 B.C.

Page 8 (inset). The Alhambra, palace and fortress of Moorish kings, in Granada. The palace was built between A.D. 1238 and 1358. After the Moors were driven away in 1492, King Charles V rebuilt parts of the Alhambra.

Page 10. *Sea Battle Between the Spanish Armada and English Naval Forces.* This oil on canvas was painted by Hendrik Cornelisz around 1600, and is now in the Landesmuseum Ferdinandeum, Innsbruck, Austria.

Page 10 (inset). "A Republican Soldier." Photographed by Robert Capa in August or September 1936, during the Spanish Civil War.

Page 11. Coat of arms of Christopher Columbus. The crest appears on a page in the *Book of Privileges* given to Columbus by King Ferdinand and Queen Isabella of Spain in 1493. The crest shows the Castle of Castile, the lion of León, an island group, and five anchors of the admiralty.

Page 18 (top). Title page from the first edition of *Don Quixote* by Miguel de Cervantes, 1605.

Page 18 (bottom). *Guernica,* painted by Pablo Picasso in 1937, after the bombing of the Basque town in the Spanish Civil War. Today the painting is displayed in the Prado Museum.

Page 19. *The Sleep of Reason Produces Monsters,* from *Los Caprichos,* plate 43. Francisco José de Goya made this etching in 1797–98, and it is in the collection of the Victoria and Albert Museum, London, England.

Web Sites

Due to the changing nature of Internet links, PowerKids Press has developed an online list of Web sites related to the subject of this book. This site is updated regularly. Please use this link to access the list:
www.powerkidslinks.com/cwpsj/pspain/